WEALTH JOURNEY

The Promise and Perils of Intergenerational Wealth

Paul Weme

Principal | Weme Consulting

Copyright © 2024

All Rights Reserved

No part of this publication may be reproduced, stored in a retrieval system, or transmitted in any form or by any means, electronic, mechanical, photocopying, recording, or otherwise, without the written permission of the author or the publisher.

Table of Contents

Acknowledgments 5

Dedication 7

Foreword 1

Introduction 4

Personal Observations from a Philanthropist and Fundraiser 9

What is a Healthy Inheritance? 15

Training A Generation Of Good Stewards 21

Living Generously 31

Discovering Your Charitable Purpose 38

How to Distribute Your Money Well 46

Conclusion 53

List of Resources 55

Appendix 1: Charity Analysis Chart 57

Appendix 2: Where to Give Next 60

Author's Notes 62

Acknowledgments

I would be remiss if I did not thank a few people who have helped get this book to its final stages.

For Mark Bakken who inspired me to write this book, and for all my friends who lent me their ear and gave me their opinions during this journey — I am eternally grateful.

Dedication

This book is dedicated to all donors who have brought me joy in my lifelong career as a Fundraiser. Also, to my wife, Shirley, my companion, and my family for their love and encouragement these number of years.

Foreword

A Second Look at What We Leave Behind

By the Honourable Gerry St Germain, Senator (RETD) P.C. O.B.C.

Generosity is a virtue. But according to historians, every generation since the Second World War has become less generous than the one before. My parents, for example, struggled to make ends meet for our family, yet they always gave what they could out of what little they had. More than any wealth they could have passed down, the life lessons that came from the example of their hard work and generosity have ended up being my true inheritance.

At the same time generosity is decreasing, and the accumulation of wealth has increased. That means more and more young people are set to inherit considerable sums of money—but do they have the generous spirit and strength of character to use it well?

Real wealth is determined not by the money we earn or inherit, but by how effectively we *use* that money. In a time when consumerism, major displays of wealth and dramatic income inequality have displaced lives of character, my hope for readers—and their families—is that they would choose to be one of the few who buck the trends and exhibit a life of generosity.

Because the truth is, we have nothing of tangible value or worldly substance left when we leave this realm. We leave with the same things we had the moment we were born. Between the beginning and the end of life, hopefully, we have learned a few things and grown to understand that our life's purpose was not just about caring for our own comforts during that journey.

One thing I've learned is that the wonderful blessings of a fulfilling family life, including both the comfort, joys, and security of loving family relationships and the responsibilities of caring for our family members, are the true sources of riches.

Once I knew my family was well cared for, I recognized I was blessed with an abundance of success. I began to explore what more I could do to help the wider community with both my material wealth and wealth of opportunity. I knew that simply showering the excess I'd been given to my children would not serve them well in the long run; in fact, it could jeopardize the very relationships and responsibilities that made my life most worth living. Instead, I chose to use my material wealth as well as my time and experience to serve the community through public service. Helping my fellow citizens and my country became a way of giving back from the overflow I was able to earn.

However, earning and managing wealth in a way that best meets our family's needs and ensures we can wisely and fruitfully give to our wider community is not always easy. It takes strategic thinking and intentional planning. It takes clear communication with our heirs, building purposeful relationships with charities and organizations, and time to reflect on our values and callings.

But the results are worth it. By ensuring wealth isn't squandered through inattention or the assumption that family should inherit everything, we can help give that hand up to someone in need, start a community project that ensures we progress as a society, or bring much-needed stability to a charity making a real difference in our world.

Each of our lives is enriched when society progresses and people can overcome disadvantages. And each of us needs to realize we *can* make a difference in our communities. This book is the first step in making sure those of us who have been given more than we need can do just that.

Introduction

In my 30-plus years as a professional fundraiser, I have seen firsthand how family philanthropy has empowered charities: those organizations whose aim is to better their community and beyond for present and future generations. I have been encouraged by the way those with financial means have used their wealth to significantly and strategically care for the world around them. I have been impressed by people who come to me with questions about how to maximize their giving today while also wanting to maximize their generational success tomorrow. They do not want to see their family wealth drift away from its potential to provide service to others.

This booklet is designed specifically with these people in mind. In it, I aim to:

- **Reduce the risk of wealth drift.**
- **Strengthen, encourage, and challenge** those who want to be strategic in their giving in a way that lines up with their passions while fulfilling their heart's desire to see generational success in their family.

- **Shine a light** on the importance of the estate planning process to show the potential for transformative impact.
- **Share personal observations and experiences** regarding philanthropy and financial stewardship that I have gathered over the past three decades.
- **Help resource charities** for a brighter world.
- **Facilitate harmony and health** for families in Canada and around the world.

Family philanthropy has an important role to play in empowering charities to do their much-needed work, and those with means have the opportunity to invest significantly in individuals and organizations committed to doing work that serves the community without reliance on profit.

Yet over the past few years, an emerging trend threatens the long-term sustainability of these charities. As donors age and begin to consider wealth transition to the next generation, some are choosing to leave greater and greater wealth to their children and grandchildren rather than to the causes and organizations that align with their values and objectives. I often hear, "I want to help my family and make sure my children are looked after," or "I want to help them have a better life." Unfortunately, the data shows that the opposite is usually the result.[1] Over and over I see that the lives of children and grandchildren who inherit significant wealth are not better. Because they have not earned the money themselves, these heirs often do not know how to manage it wisely. Wealth poorly stewarded negatively impacts families themselves, as well as the

---

[1] Some estimate that up to 70% of wealth is lost by the second generation. The number rises to 90% by the third generation. "Generational Wealth: Why do 70% of Families Lose Their Wealth in the 2nd Generation?" nasdaq.com, October 19, 2018, www.nasdaq.com/articles/generational-wealth%3A-why-do-70-of-families-lose-their-wealth-in-the-2nd-generation-2018-10

community, as fewer funds are devoted toward transformational philanthropy. This is especially true today when fewer lower- and middle-income people are choosing to donate to charity, leaving the sector more reliant on donors with means (see Chapter 4).

Reflecting on this issue, I was reminded of a book called *Mission Drift* by Peter Greer. The book discusses how to keep non-profit organizations from drifting away from their mission. I thought, yes, that is happening in some families with intergenerational wealth. Just as Greer's book focuses on why and how to avoid mission drift, this booklet discusses how and why to avoid wealth drift—the movement of wealth away from one's passions, values, and personal mission toward areas where it can be squandered or, worse, actively harm.

There is hope. With careful and open estate planning and a healthy transition of wealth, your family can protect itself against wealth drift. Not only will your whole family be healthier and happier, but you will have peace in knowing that you have lived a life aligned with your values that has made a lasting difference in the world. If done well, your legacy can have an impact that your family will honor and follow for generations.

I've worked with several organizations over the years, and it broke my heart to see the power wealth had to destroy families and distort people's desires. But the more I've shared the ideas in this book with others, I've learned that many are hungry for tools to manage their wealth in a way that benefits both their neighbors and their heirs. I strongly believe the actions we take in this life and the way we steward our wealth can have long-lasting value. But that principle is true for all people in the extraordinary position to disperse significant amounts of money: through our choices, we can make decisions whose effects reverberate far beyond our lifetime.

Keep reading if you want to learn how to leverage your wealth for a profound benefit to both your family and the world around you—for generations to come.

- Paul Weme (Langley, BC)

Chapter 1

Personal Observations from a Philanthropist and Fundraiser

Many people I have worked with over the years have shared the same observation with me: that our parents' and grandparents' generations recognized the importance of giving. They honored the call—one that, for many, was rooted in deeply held faith convictions—to give and to give generously. They recognized that no matter how little they had, there was always someone with less. The Greatest Generation (born in the early 20th century) had very little to give but still gave generously. As subsequent generations built wealth, the ethic of generosity was well instilled. Recent research backs this up: though the number of the Greatest Generation is shrinking, a 2018 Blackbaud report shows they still give the most per capita. Baby Boomers, the current "grandparent" generation, are not far behind.

Many of these individuals represent the first or second generation to build significant assets that could be passed on to families. Some started with little in life, worked hard, and saved scrupulously. In addition, a number from this generation created successful businesses, benefited from the real estate boom or wisely capitalized on a more global economy.

In 1999, the Social Welfare Research Institute at Boston College reported that there would be a $41 trillion intergenerational wealth transfer in the US over the next 55 years (i.e., by 2054). In Canada, the Toronto-based firm Strategic Insight notes that, as I write this book, we are in the midst of the largest-ever recorded transfer of intergenerational wealth, with more than $1 trillion projected to be passed on to the next generation from 2016 to 2026.[2] That is a staggering amount of money being inherited by children and grandchildren.

---

[2] Investment Planning Counsel, "Affluent Canadians are worried about wealth transfer," newswire.ca, Cision, January 30, 2018, https://www.newswire.ca/news-releases/affluent-canadians-are-worried-about-wealth-transfer-671751984.html

While the potential for good from this wealth transfer is immense, there is also risk. The generous spirit shown by our elders is not always passed on to second and third generations, particularly when heirs receive unearned wealth. Well-meaning parents may have failed to model good stewardship because they did not want to "let the right hand know what the left hand is doing," and therefore did not share their approaches to giving with their families. Yet by keeping *why* they give a secret, they have inadvertently prevented their children and grandchildren from knowing the joy of generosity. In addition, parents who didn't come from money themselves may, despite having a comfortable amount of wealth, not fully understand their position to influence the world for good through family philanthropy.

> *"We make a living by what we get, but we make a life by what we give."*
>
> *- Winston Churchill*

Notice we are never encouraged to be a "cheerful leaver." Yet that is precisely what more and more parents are doing—leaving the bulk of the wealth they have amassed to their children and grandchildren without careful thought about considering the transformational good that money could do elsewhere. How do we ensure that the next generation will not squander money they did not earn, treating their inheritance more like a lottery win than a responsibility?

Today in Canada, inheritances typically come at a time when the beneficiaries live separately from their parents, have careers, are financially independent, and already have what they need. These beneficiaries are rarely carrying on the family business; if they are, they do not need a financial windfall to do so. They have dependable sources of income generated by their own work, skills, savings, and investing.

When such people inherit a farm, house, or other real estate, what becomes of it? Typically, the asset is liquidated or used as a further source of income . . . but is not needed. Having it simply increases the heirs' standard of living, sometimes dramatically. But having that much wealth does not guarantee these upcoming generations will be as generous as the parents who left it to them or give to the causes their parents were passionate about. Above all, it does not mean they will live happy, purpose-filled lives.

Unfortunately, in my experience working with hundreds of high-net-worth families, the hope that children will use the money they inherit for charitable purposes seldom pans out. By the time intergenerational wealth gets to the third generation, charitable giving is often non-existent. Forbes Magazine reported in 2018 that "more than 70 percent of estate transfers failed to complete the hopes of those leaving it behind." This is wealth drift.

> *"The greatest use of life is to spend it for something that will outlast it."*
>
> *- William James*

Despite the arguments against it, I see more and more people deciding to give their full fortunes to their children, an unfortunate pattern that does double harm. First, they may hurt their family by giving them unearned wealth that can be detrimental to their integrity, particularly if they do not understand the responsibilities that come with wealth. Second, they are not engaging in the wisdom of previous generations and their cultural traditions: that generosity is a core component of a life well lived that leads to a stronger society and personal happiness.

If you have more wealth than you need to live well, you have an extraordinary opportunity to help fuel the engine that drives charities and organizations in service of the greater good. This is a joy-filled privilege! It is also a practice that can grow gratitude in your own life, intimacy among your family, and flourishing in your community.

I believe it is more than possible for intentional planning to ensure that familial wealth can benefit the world around us without jeopardizing family relationships. A purposeful, happy life is guided by gratitude for all we have been given. This gratitude is what can motivate us to lead lives that culminate in a legacy of generosity that outlives us.

Chapter 2

What is a Healthy Inheritance?

Defining a healthy inheritance can be difficult. As humans, we have a normal and loving desire to give to our children. On the other hand, many of us accept that those who have inherited or created great wealth have an obligation to use it for the good of others outside our immediate family. Being wise with our financial resources means holding both these truths at the same time.

The two are not mutually exclusive: I do not believe we should give to charities and nonprofits at the expense of our families. Nor should we give to our families at the expense of charities. However, for those who have an abundance of wealth, the question gets complicated. How much is "enough" when it comes to caring for our family members? And how can we ensure the wealth we pass on does not harm our children? What exactly *is* a healthy inheritance?

Let me share examples of how wealth transfer, based on my own experiences, was done well and how it was done poorly.

In the first example, Jonathan had amassed great wealth. He wanted to make sure his children got started on the right foot in life and assisted each of them with buying a house as well as helping to pay for his grandchildren's education. When asked by his children if he would help pay for his great-grandchildren's education, he declined, saying that financially helping his great-grandchildren was up to his children, not him.

Jonathan was open with his children from an early age and much of his wealth would go to support philanthropy. He set an example for his children by sharing where he gave money and why—eventually inviting them to participate in meetings and decision-making regarding his charitable giving, so they had a solid foundation to become generous themselves.

Once Jonathan's children were mature enough, he gave them each a sum that would be their inheritance. He added the stipulation that the money go toward charitable causes. Because he had instilled in them a vision to use their wealth for the good of others, they were excited to develop their charitable purpose and see their father's wealth continue to power causes about which he was passionate.

In the second example, David and Delores had also amassed great wealth. They too helped their children buy homes and paid for their grandchildren's education. However, instead of giving a set amount of money to their children and being an open example of generosity for their families, they divided their total wealth among their children. This lump sum was given to each child at an age before they were mature and responsible enough to spend the money wisely, and the couple did not put any stipulations on how they expected the money to be spent. David and Delores' children spent the money on second homes and material items, living in luxury. Only a few years after receiving the inheritance, each of David and Delores' children admitted they were not satisfied with their lives, and much of the wealth was gone.

"Don't handicap your children by making their lives easy."
- Robert A. Heinlein

Jonathan's legacy shines bright, while David and Delores squandered the opportunity to make a transformative impact through their wealth.

No two families are alike. We each have children with differing levels of maturity, interests, and lifestyles. Some families have loads of grandchildren all attending expensive universities, while others have fewer expenses and simpler tastes. Regardless of your situation, there are a few principles to keep in mind if you plan to give a healthy inheritance:

1. Tell your children from an early age that they should not expect to inherit all your wealth. Help them understand that this choice is for both their benefit and for organizations doing exceptional work.
2. Be open with your children about the pitfalls and opportunities that come with great wealth. Help them understand that wealth is not a birthright; it is an enormous responsibility.
3. Do not give large sums of money to children who are too young to manage it wisely or to live meaningful and satisfying lives regardless of their financial situation. Timing is key. Remember: young adult brains, particularly the prefrontal cortex, which helps us control impulsivity and organize our lives, are not fully mature until our mid-20s!
4. Instead of handing over a blank check, openly communicate your wishes for how you would like your children to use the inheritance they receive. If you want your funds to continue working for the good of the world after you are gone, designate that a percentage—or all—of the money you give must be given to charity or nonprofit.

5. Engage your family in estate planning and involve them in your charitable activities. Share the passions of your heart and talk with them about their own charitable vision. The National Christian Foundation uses the language of "invitation": "Invite your family into a meaningful, open conversation about your vision for your estate's legacy today, as well as tomorrow."[3]
6. Above all, focus on giving your children an inheritance that is more than money. Help them build lives of character—not just when it comes to financial accountability, but regarding living with integrity, compassion, and humility. Demonstrate these values in your own life by spending thoughtfully and finding joy in things not related to status or wealth. At the same time, prioritize your personal relationship by showing your love for them in ways that do not involve money or luxury—particularly through quality time together.

If you have raised mature, healthy children who are secure in your love for them and who understand that happiness does not come

---

[3] Eric Most, "A generous legacy today and tomorrow with estate gifts," ncfgiving.com, National Christian Foundation, Jan. 7, 2023, https://tinyurl.com/yx5ryvku

from material things, you can confidently pass on your wealth with great joy!

It is good and right to include your children in your will and to use your wealth to give them a solid footing in life. It is also good and right to give your money away. With a well-rounded vision for your life, these two things need not be in conflict. Generosity can help bring unity and purpose to your family. It can strengthen family bonds and help each individual see that they play a role in a vision of life that is much bigger than their desires and comfort.

We cannot control the outcomes of our actions. But we can live in a way that considers the health not just of our pocketbooks but of our children's hearts. If you have abundance beyond your own needs, I hope this chapter helps you give careful and strategic thought about not only how to divide your estate, but how to leave a legacy that lives on through your children.

Chapter 3

Training A Generation Of Good Stewards

Once we have decided to leave a healthy inheritance, how do we actually train our children to steward it well?

This is a critical question that too few are asking. In 2017, a private wealth company asked high-net-worth individuals how much they had communicated with their children about wealth transfer. The poll revealed that 58 percent had yet to discuss any plans about their estate with their kids or other heirs—12 percent never planned to talk to them at all! In a separate question, 32 percent said they were "worried about how their heirs will handle their inheritance"; another 36 percent said their children "don't have the financial literacy to manage a potential windfall."[4]

---

[4] Investment Planning Counsel, "Affluent Canadians are worried about wealth transfer."

How do we buck these trends and prepare our children to be good stewards of their financial inheritance? How do we talk to our children about the charitable aspects of our life?

As I mentioned in the first chapter, many older generations have a mindset that "the right hand should not know what the left is doing." When I ask older donors if their children know where they give, the answer is, "Of course not!" This humility comes from a good place, but it is critical to remember that parenting is not a business transaction—it is a lifelong commitment to love and equip our children in all areas of their lives, including generosity and giving. As parents, we are our children's first and best teachers. If we do not teach them, many other people are waiting in the wings to influence their desires, spending habits, and lifestyles.

Instead of encouraging modesty, avoiding talking to our children about wealth and generosity can encourage unhealthy expectations as to what will happen when the parents die. Children tend to feel that the inheritance is "owed" somehow. But no one is owed great wealth. Countless examples show that wealth can go as easily as it comes. Stock markets fall, real estate busts and loans don't get paid back. None of these are things we can control. Before we can prepare our children to be good stewards of our—and their own—

financial means, we need to give them a strong foundation not just for what to expect from us, but why.

"You have to teach your children values like humility, gratitude, and kindness, not entitlement and privilege."

- Tony Dungy

From a young age, we should focus on providing our children with three values:

1. A work ethic: Give them the skills and integrity to make their own way in the world so they are not dependent on a full inheritance to live meaningful lives.
2. Financial literacy: Train your children specifically in how to manage affluence. It is a learned skill set!
3. Value capital: Train them in core human values so they inherit an attitude of generosity and excitement to do good in the world with any funds they do have.

Russ Crosson, President of Ronald Blue & Co., sums it up well: "If we produce children that are productive and content . . . it almost doesn't matter how much we leave them. If our children are consumptive and discontent, we won't be able to leave them enough." When you give exorbitant wealth to your children without providing them with the social, practical, and ethical resources to handle it, you put them in a dangerous position.

In my work, I see this most poignantly when it comes to family relationships, which money can easily get in the way of. I have met families where the generations are estranged due to the consequences of great wealth. Aside from dealing with the broken relationships that should be the most meaningful in their lives, parents in this situation must recognize that their children are unlikely to use their inheritance well.

A few common questions about leaving money to children

What if one or some of my children do not share my values?

If you desire that some of the wealth you give to your children should go to causes you care about, you might feel conflicted if one of your children does not share your religious, political, or social views. This can be difficult to navigate, but here are a few thoughts.

- Regardless of whether you align with your child on important topics, take time to engage him or her in conversations about philanthropy and generosity. You can still be aligned with them when it comes to the importance

of foundational values like generosity and a desire to benefit others, even if these beliefs are expressed in different ways.
- Model a life that recognizes true happiness does not come simply from owning great wealth, but from using it well.
- This also gets to my most important point: live out your charitable purpose in your lifetime (see Chapter 5) so you are not reliant on your children to do it for you. Give them social and ethical capital, plus a reasonable inheritance that makes sense for your family—but do not leave it to them to do your life's work.

Should I give the same amount of money to every child?

The answer to this depends on each family. Some parents may know their children well enough to realize keeping everything even will promote peace and healthy relationships after they are gone. Others might want to leave money based on where each child's current life situation or the level of maturity or responsibility each child shows.

Randy Alcorn recommends the second approach: "The question is not what is fair, but what is right. The real questions are, will your children need your money and will they use it wisely? If the answer to the first question is no, then you should not feel compelled to leave it to them. If the answers markedly differ from child to child, then you should deal differently with them according to those real differences."[5]

Alcorn makes a good point, but what you choose will ultimately be influenced by your personality and your family's values. Regardless of your plan, **communication is key**. Be open and honest with your children, and invite them to be open with you. This builds trust and respect that protects families against the petty in-fighting that can result when it comes to inheritances.

How can I encourage generosity in my children when they are young?

Start small! Young children love to be generous. Perhaps at Christmas, you could select a few charities for your children to decide between to give a family gift. You could regularly take children to volunteer so they are exposed to people without great wealth and see firsthand how donations make a difference. You could sponsor a child of a similar age and take time to learn about their culture, language, and life experience.

---

[5] Randy Alcorn, *Money, Possessions, and Eternity*, Tyndale House Publishers: 2021.

When my kids were young, my wife and I gave them a small allowance, ten percent of which they had to set aside to give away. We did not require them to give it to a particular cause. They were able to choose a cause that excited their hearts.

Another time, we took our kids on a family trip to Latin America. We wanted them to see firsthand why we support the charities working there. As a family, we helped paint houses, ran school programs, and served in an orphanage. I had been to Guatemala several times before, so it was exciting to introduce my family to some of the orphans I had worked with.

We loved meeting with the locals, learning about the culture and building relationships with some of the people in the region! Beyond that, we were able to expose our children to intentional acts of kindness, involve them in charitable work beyond giving, and share the driving passions of our hearts with them.

Even the smallest actions can sow the seeds of generosity in a child's heart.

How can I nurture generosity in teenagers?

Older kids are ready to take on more responsibility. In my experience as a parent of teens, I've learned that as they age, you become more of a coach and less of a boss. That makes the teen years the perfect time to begin having regular "coaching" conversations about money—and not just about generosity. Tell them why and how you chose to make a big purchase like a car, and even ask them if they would do something differently!

Consider giving them a small amount of money to give away. Show them how you choose a charity, talk through the pros and cons of giving one large gift versus spreading it among more organizations, and share what to expect when you give to charity. Make sure you have some quality time together unrelated to a specific purpose so they can begin to tell you about the passions in their own hearts.

Finally, start having conversations now about the expectations they should have regarding your financial role in their lives. What can they expect from you in terms of their education, buying a home, or starting a business? What should they be prepared to contribute? You should also start having open, age-appropriate conversations about their inheritance. They may not be ready to talk about the reality that you will pass away one day—but the earlier they realize you are not planning to give them all of your wealth, the better.

How can I talk to adult children about wealth, particularly if we are not used to having these types of conversations?

Consider a small project you could work on with each of your children to be generous together. A dear friend of mine recently did this. He invited his three adult sons, all in their 30s, to talk with him and his wife about their next year of giving. He asked each son to help him decide where to donate $50,000, within certain parameters. Note that his children are grown, but it wasn't too late to start!

This model is a beautiful example of how parents can involve their children in giving, set realistic expectations, and participate together in caring for others.

If you and your children are not used to having open conversations about difficult topics, begin to actively seek out opportunities to repair relationships and open up the lines of communication. Be honest about where you might need to ask for forgiveness or adjust your expectations or interactions with your kids. As long as we're alive, it's not too late to repair broken relationships, although such repair is only possible when we are willing to be humble, listen, and make small steps toward change.

Teaching your kids—no matter how much money you have

The truth is, all of these tips apply whether we are high-net-worth individuals or not. Generosity is not limited to those with means. It is a posture of our hearts toward others. An ethic of generosity is something we cannot just talk about: it is something we do. When you align your financial life with your values, your kids will notice, no matter their age!

Chapter 4

Living Generously

Why be generous? For some, it may seem to be a straightforward question. For others, the answer could be more complicated. Maybe generosity was not modeled to you as a young person. Maybe the problems of the world feel so overwhelming that you do not see how your contributions can make a difference. Maybe you worry about shrinking your portfolio to a degree that makes you uncomfortable. You may be thinking: it's my money. Isn't generosity optional for living a good life?

Throughout the centuries, however, the wisest voices across cultures have been united in a belief that generosity is not just important, it's crucial.

Let's start with religion. While the major religions of the world diverge on many important points, all share one aspect in common: a conviction that without generosity, it is impossible to live a wholehearted life of love.

Many world religions show special consideration for the poor by including regular almsgiving as a major tenet. In the Jewish scriptures, Israel is consistently held accountable for how it treats the lowliest in society, including children, widows, and those without means. In the New Testament, Jesus speaks regularly about God's heart for the poor—those lacking in both material and spiritual resources. This call to be generous is foundational in many Eastern religions as well, including Buddhism and Sikhism.[6] Whether or not one is a person of faith, the collective wisdom of these religious traditions is that *generosity matters.* Most major religions represented in Canada, including Christianity, Judaism, and Islam, base this conviction on the premise that earthly possessions, including wealth, are gifts from God that must be stewarded, not things over which one has full ownership.

"You can give without loving, but you cannot love without giving."
- Amy Carmichael

---

[6] See the Lake Institute for the latest research and invaluable insights on the strong relationship between faith and giving: https://lakeinstitute.org/.

Contemporary research backs up these ancient insights. It turns out that giving to others—whether donating to charity, giving person to person, or sharing our time and talent—is not just a nice thing to do: it actively benefits our emotional and physical health. Giving has been linked to lower blood pressure, reduced inflammation, and less stress, all factors that can influence our sense of physical well-being and even help us live longer. People who give to charity also have a greater sense of connection to their community, which is of utmost importance in our day of increasing loneliness and disconnection.[7]

Instead of focusing on scarcity and competition, generosity allows us to step back from our consumer culture and appreciate what we already have. Generosity can turn our gaze outward, away from ourselves, giving us a larger and more satisfying perspective on the world. By promoting stronger social ties, giving can also be a catalyst for healthier, more unified societies that are prepared to tackle issues that far outpace what one individual can do alone.

---

[7] Jason Marsh and Jill Suttie, "Five Ways Giving Is Good for You," *Greater Good Magazine,* UC Berkeley, December 13, 2010: https://greatergood.berkeley.edu/article/item/5_ways_giving_is_good_for_you

Finally, giving makes us feel *happy*. A 2008 study by Elizabeth Dunn, a happiness researcher at the University of British Columbia, showed that giving money to charities increased the level of happiness people felt. On the other hand, the study found that "money spent on personal expenses or new stuff had no effect on a person's happiness levels."[8] At the same time, the 2022 World Happiness Report found that "donating money is one of the six strongest predictors of life satisfaction"—even after controlling for other measures of wealth and prosperity.[9]

> *"No one has ever become poor by giving."*
> *- Anne Frank*

Unfortunately, despite the strong links between generosity and personal and social well-being, charity watchdogs have released numerous reports sounding the alarm that levels of charitable giving

---

[8] Elizabeth W. Dunn, Lara B. Akin, Michael I. Norton." Spending Money on Others Promotes Happiness." *Science* 21 March 2008: Vol. 319, Issue 5870, pp. 1687-1688, as referenced by Markham Heid, "Why Giving to Causes You Care About is Good for Your Health," Everyday Health, September 20, 2023, https://www.everydayhealth.com/emotional-health/why-giving-to-causes-you-care-about-is-good-for-your-health/

[9] Heid, "Why Giving to Causes You Care About"

in Canada are decreasing. The Fraser Institute's 2023 Generosity Index reports that both the number of Canadians giving to charity and the average percentage of annual income people give have fallen steadily in the past decade, a trend that was exacerbated by the COVID-19 pandemic. As the report states, "This decline in generosity in Canada undoubtedly limits the ability of Canadian charities to improve the quality of life in their communities and beyond."[10]

There are numerous reasons for this trend. Some of it is explained by the generational shifts we discussed earlier. The Ontario Nonprofit Network ties the decline to the soaring cost of living and increased inflation. Many people are feeling economic pressures as basic needs, like housing and groceries, become less affordable. Canada Helps, in their 2023 Giving Report, also notes that increasing social disconnection has impacted people's willingness to give. "As a society, we have become increasingly disconnected and isolated, and as a result, it is harder than ever for individuals to see their role in making change," the report summarizes.[11] Finally, many

---

[10] "Generosity in Canada: The 2023 Generosity Index," The Fraser Institute, December 2023.

[11] "The Giving Report 2023," Canadahelps, December 2023.

agree that decreasing religiosity also contributes to this downward trend. This decrease in giving has, unfortunately, coincided with an increase in people turning to charities to make ends meet.[12]

Despite the decrease in the number of donors, the total value of donations has actually increased. This means a smaller number of donors are responsible for upholding a critical sector in our society, putting the sustainability of many charities at risk—particularly those that do not attract larger gifts, such as small, grassroots organizations. This fact provides even more of a challenge for those with the means to respond with generosity to the opportunities around them.

An invitation to live generously

Living generously is not something we *must* do out of guilt or fear of social reprisals. It is a commitment that betters one's own self and the world around us, backed by the depth of wisdom stemming from ancient religious traditions and contemporary research on

---

[12] "Charitable Giving has reached a Historic Low in Canada—Now What?" The Ontario Non-Profit Network, August 31, 2023, https://theonn.ca/2023/08/charitable-giving-has-reached-a-historic-low-in-canada-now-what/; https://www.statcan.gc.ca/o1/en/plus/5288-how-your-donations-matter-what-non-profit-organizations-are-telling-us.

well-being. Giving is not something to do begrudgingly. Once you realize the benefits, giving is truly a great joy!

"Generosity is the most natural outward expression of an inner attitude of compassion and loving-kindness."

- The Dalai Lama XIV

Chapter 5

Discovering Your Charitable Purpose

One of the main messages I want you to take away from this booklet is that the best thing you can do to protect against wealth drift is to intentionally plan your wealth distribution in your lifetime.

But you cannot intentionally distribute your wealth if you have not thought about what you want your wealth to do in this world.

I believe every person has a passion that has been laid on their heart. This could be to build wells in Africa or to feed the homeless in our own backyards. It could be to help researchers make discoveries that can relieve suffering or protect the environment for the sake of future generations.

The best way to live a full and meaningful life is to align our passions with our actions. As a person with means, one of the top actions you can take is setting aside money to give away to causes that stir your heart while benefiting others.

"If you can't feed a hundred people, then just feed one."
- Mother Teresa

Sadly, this is not the case with many donors. When I ask them why they give, they mention that something was a parent's favorite cause or a gift was given as a favor for a friend. Some feel disillusioned with the charities they give to or feel taken advantage of (more on this in Chapter 6). Too many do not feel the joy or sense of purpose that should accompany generous giving.

Does this sound like you?

Before I walk you through four steps to discern your charitable purpose, I want to make a quick note about husbands and wives. For married couples, it is critical not to neglect your spouse in these conversations. Men are still overwhelmingly the lead decision-makers on financial decisions (74 percent of households[13]), yet statistically, most wives will outlive their husbands and be responsible for dealing with the couple's estate. In addition, I still

---

[13] Investment Planning Counsel, "Affluent Canadians are worried about wealth transfer."

come across men who assume their wives do not care about giving or have no charitable passions of their own.

This is unfortunate! It is a great source of joy in marriage when we can be unified in a common cause and act generously together. It goes without saying that women have passions and causes they want to support, yet many are not given the opportunity to share them in marriages where they are not equal financial partners. By working together on giving, you strengthen your marital bond through your shared purpose, and you can experience the joy of supporting each other's deepest passions and callings.

Finally, on a practical note, when a spouse is unaware of your vision for giving or your wealth in general, he or she will be unequipped to distribute the family fortune well once the primary decision-maker has died. The most likely result is that he or she will simply pass on the full estate to children—allowing the wealth to drift.

Four steps to discerning your charitable purpose

There is a good chance that you know deep inside whether or not you are satisfied with your current giving. It is good to recognize this feeling if you have it. But even if you know you are not living in alignment with your values, how do you discern what that charitable purpose is in the first place? Here are the steps I guide my clients through.

1. Write your life Purpose Statement.

Most organizations—whether for-profit or non-profit—start with a mission statement. Some spend thousands of dollars working with consultants to create one. Why? Without a mission statement, it can be difficult to act with intention and make decisions that align with your values. Why should we expect less for our charitable lives?

For individuals, the first step I always recommend in discerning your charitable purpose is writing a life purpose statement. For example, a life purpose statement could be "I want every act I take to promote peacemaking," or "my life exists to make this world better for my great-grandchildren."

Once you have a statement written down, you now have a powerful assessment tool: "Will this charitable donation promote peace?" "Will this purchase help maintain the world for future generations?" If the answer is no, then you know not to move forward.

Writing a life purpose statement might not feel productive—but it is the most important step to ensure your giving has the impact you desire. Take some time, alone or with your spouse, to write a simple life purpose statement that can guide the rest of your answers.

2. Reflect on the passions of your heart.

Set aside time to reflect on the types of giving that charge your heart. This could be writing down moments that have been pivotal in your life, naming people or organizations that inspire you, or reflecting on day-to-day experiences or news stories you cannot get out of your head.

Keep a long document where you can "brain dump" your ideas. Once you have quite a few, schedule some quiet time to reflect on the list. When you see them all together, what rises to the top? Do one or two items jump off the page? Are there any themes you see over and over again, like education, poverty relief, or conservation? Read a few out loud—does your heart or gut respond a certain way? Be curious and non-judgmental about what rises to the top. The answers may surprise you!

If you are married, consider doing this exercise separately and comparing lists. Where are your hearts unified? If there are differences, which areas can you joyfully support from the other person's list?

In addition, consider asking a trusted friend what types of causes or ideas you tend to talk about unprompted. Sometimes an outside observer can notice things that are difficult to see for ourselves.

"It takes generosity to discover the whole through others. If you realize you are only a violin, you can open yourself up to the world by playing your role in the concert."

- Jacques-Yves Cousteau

3. Analyze your current giving.

Now it is time to take an honest look at the giving you are already doing.

When I work with donors, I ask them to make a simple chart (See Appendix 1 for an example). At the top of the page, write down the top passions you have identified in your reflection process. Next, create a list of the charities you have given to in the past three to five years. Next to each charity, write down whether or not they align with any of your passions, the accountability you have experienced from the charity, and the outcomes they have reported from your gift.

Now, you can ask yourself a few questions:

- What gifts have you given that have aligned with your life purpose statement? Which have not?
- What charities do you support that align with your discerned passions?
- Which gifts have led to outcomes that support your life purpose and passions?
- Which charities are stewarding your donation well?

If there is a significant disconnect between your life purpose statement and your current giving, you now have helpful data to make better giving decisions.

4. Make the most of where you give.

Now that you have some information to make more intentional decisions in the future, it is time to start selecting places to invest your money in the outcomes you would like to see in the world. I ask you to be open to where this could take you. Be willing to stretch yourself and consider projects in new areas or with longer timelines. I want you to feel a deep sense of excitement and possibility, even if it means adjusting your mindset, going against the grain, or taking on new risks.

It is important to note that this is not a static process. As we grow in maturity and life experience, our heart passions will evolve as well. This is not bad—it is much worse to get stuck in a giving rut and only distribute money "because that is what I have always done." I recommend going through this reflection and analysis process at least once a year. Do not be afraid to change your mind and your relationships over time.

As usual, make this process transparent to your children. Be honest with them about your heart's desire for your wealth—better yet, share the stories and experiences through which you have discerned these passions in your heart. In doing so, you will set a priceless example and grow a meaningful relationship with your loved ones. You may even spark similar passions in them.

Chapter 6

How to Distribute Your Money Well

At the end of the day, I want people with the means to see their money as a precious gift that they have the tremendous opportunity to invest for the greater good of the world. This is not an opportunity (or a responsibility) everyone gets to experience!

One way you can live up to this formidable but rewarding invitation is to treat your money as an investment: with a focus on accountability, outcomes, balanced risk, and strategy. The return is not in more wealth or prestige—it is an investment in your own legacy, your family's virtue, and the greater good. People who manage wealth tend to spend significant time planning, executing, and analyzing their investment strategies, particularly if those investments can grow their financial returns. However, true wealth—including a purposeful life, meaningful relationships, and a lasting legacy aligned with our values—is not found in money. Shouldn't our efforts and excitement toward investments with nonfinancial returns match or even exceed what we devote to our regular portfolios?

Donor dollars are the fuel for charity and can make a huge difference in the world. But, as noted earlier, any funds that trickle down to subsequent generations are far more likely to drift away from your vision and passion.

"Every man must decide whether he will walk in the light of creative altruism or in the darkness of destructive selfishness."
- Martin Luther King, Jr.

Here are my tips for giving money away well, both in your lifetime and through your estate:

1. Give money away in your lifetime

Following the invitation to align your passions with the actions you take, I encourage you to enthusiastically give wealth away in your own lifetime instead of storing it up to generate more wealth for yourself or your children. This can be difficult for some, particularly those who earned their wealth slowly and may still have a scarcity mindset regarding their money; or for first-generation high-net-worth individuals who are not aware of the transformative potential of a significant gift in the right hands.

While everyone will have different preferences for how they give, this encouragement has implications for how much we commit to donor-advised funds and endowments. There is an important place for both of these tools in the world of philanthropy. While they can, for example, provide invaluable sustainability for some organizations, in many cases tying up these dollars can actually limit how much good a gift can do by capping the amount of giving possible each year. Remember that when money is stored in charitable investment funds, which is true of *millions* of donor dollars today, these dollars are already no longer part of your net worth—shouldn't they be allowed to fulfill their purpose?

When you give money away instead of storing it up in regular or charitable investments, the benefits are huge. First and foremost, you ensure those dollars go toward your passion and are not at the mercy of future generations. It also gives you the chance to partner with organizations in a real and powerful way. Some examples might be providing funding to scale the growth of a particularly effective organization, purchasing equipment for desperately needed but expensive medical research, or covering the long-term overhead cost of a grassroots organization so they can deliver programs more effectively while fairly paying their staff. And you get to enjoy seeing the fruits of these investments in your lifetime!

"Give what you have. To someone, it may be better than you dare to think."

- Henry Wadsworth Longfellow

Transformative gifts are, of course, exciting. But my friend Phil recently reminded me that many donors forget that even a relatively small gift can have a huge impact if given to the right person in a key field of influence. Sometimes these "high-impact people" do not look like your typical high achievers, but they exhibit the vision and tenacity to do transformative work without huge budgets. Keep your eye out for these world-changers, and do not be afraid to take a well-planned risk.

2. Build positive relationships with charities.

As I noted previously, many donors might not be giving as vigorously as they could because they lack trust in the organization receiving their funds. Maybe they had a bad experience where funds were spent in a different way than planned and they were not notified. Perhaps they simply feel unappreciated or are not receiving reports on the impact their gift has had. Maybe they were sold an impossible outcome and the reality on the ground has been disappointing.

If you see your giving as an investment in the greater good, try to match your passions with charities that are faithful to their commitments and will be accountable for the generosity shown to them.

The key to a great relationship with a charity is to think in terms of an investment partnership. You need to thoroughly assess whether the organization is a good investment; they need to be transparent about how they operate and what they can deliver. Here are some steps that can help you assess a charity:

- Before you give, ask the organization how they will report back on how your gift has been used.
- Ask for a signed gift agreement with terms that work for both of you.
- Take time to understand the organization's mission, programs, and operations so you can have realistic expectations about delivery timelines and outcomes.
- Ask a charity to outline the challenges they face and how those might impact how your gift is used. Be wary of organizations that sugarcoat difficulties—honesty is key!

- Request that any changes regarding how the money is used be discussed with you immediately.
- Take the initiative to check in with the charity every six months to hear about their progress.
- Be wary of organizations that over-promise or claim results that are not easily verified.

Like any investment, some risk is involved. All charities share one thing in common: they are run by imperfect people who cannot tell the future. But a transparent charity will readily agree to these terms, which will help mitigate risk and bring back the joy of giving.

3. Review your estate plan every five years.

Some of us, even after an active lifetime of philanthropy, will still have an abundance to pass on after our deaths. After taking a reasonable amount of care of your family, consider well how that wealth might continue to be used for the greater good after you are gone. This could include:

- Planning a legacy gift to a beloved partner charity you worked with in your lifetime.
- Designating a local organization as a partial beneficiary of your will.

- Giving a lump sum to each child with explicit instructions for them to give the money away to causes that speak to their hearts.
- Setting up a foundation for your children to steward after your death focused on areas of support that align with your life purpose statement.

You cannot do a kindness too soon because you never know how soon it will be too late."

- Ralph Waldo Emerson

Every five years, review your plan based on your children's and grandchildren's needs upon your death, your current assets, and your relationships with partner charities, in addition to taking time to once again assess how your passions and values have evolved.

Each time you undertake this process, be explicit with your heirs about your desires and expectations. Share the passions and heart behind your decision-making—hopefully, in understanding the "why" behind your choices, they will be more inclined to respect your legacy and honor your wishes.

Conclusion

"The value of a man resides in what he gives and not in what he is capable of receiving."
- Albert Einstein

As it stands now, far too much money is wasted on intergenerational giving. Money that could have been used to make a lasting difference for present and future generations is given to family members who either do not need it or do not have the maturity or tools to steward it well.

There is a better way. As people with means, it is time to shift your mindset to one of generosity: How can you live up to the responsibility of this tremendous gift you have been given?

I hope this book challenges you to think differently about your wealth and gives you tools to live as a person of character. I invite you to enter into the joy of generosity and the peace of living a life that aligns the abundance you have at your disposal with your unique set of passions.

In the end, the path is not complicated. Be intentional about estate planning. Give money away to causes you love in your lifetime. Work with a like-minded advisor who will help you wisely put greater-good investments first. Involve your children, training them in generosity and inviting them to explore their own charitable passions.

I hope you catch the excitement and the possibility I feel as I write this book. There is so much opportunity by heeding this invitation to share our wealth: stronger bonds with loved ones, purpose-filled families, the joy of giving well, and children unburdened by unearned wealth.

The choice is yours. I invite you to embrace a wholehearted life of generosity today.

List of Resources

The Eternity Portfolio, Illuminated: A Practical Guide to Investing Your Money for Ultimate Results by Alan Gotthardt. Deep River Books: 2015.

The Giver and the Gift: Principles of Kingdom Fundraising by Peter Greer and David Weekley. Baker Publishing Group: 2015.

Giving It All Away…and Getting It All Back Again: The Way of Living Generously by David Green. Zondervan: 2017.

The Law of Rewards by Randy Alcorn. Tyndale House Publishers, Inc: 2003

Mission Drift by Peter Greer and Chris Horst. Baker Publishing Group: 2015.

Money, Possessions, and Eternity by Randy Alcorn. Tyndale House Publishers: 2021.

The Pastor's Justification: Applying the Work of Christ in Your Life and Ministry by Jared C. Wilson. Crossway: 2013.

The Treasure Principle: Revised and Updated by Randy Alcorn. Multnomah: 2012.

unHeritage: 11 Pitfalls to Family Legacy and How to Avoid Them by Tom Conway and Steve Gardner. Familybrand Press: 2014.

Appendix 1: Charity Analysis Chart

Use this chart to help analyze your current giving and its impact compared to your passions. Fill it out after reading "Discerning your charitable purpose" in Chapter 5. For a downloadable copy, visit www.wealthdrift.ca.

Year:
Life Purpose Statement:
Passions Identified: • • • • •

Charities I have given to in the past three years	Passion alignment: (Does it align with one of the bullets listed above?	Accountability: What reporting or communication have I received?	Outcomes: What impact has come from the gift?

Wealth Journey

Year:			

Appendix 2: Where to Give Next

Use this chart to help better align your next year of giving with your charitable purposes. For a downloadable copy, visit www.wealthdrift.ca.

Life Passion: What is your philanthropic story?			
Passions	Desired Outcomes	Potential Charities	Accountability

Wealth Journey

Author's Notes

Much of what I share are principals I have learned from the Bible. My desire as a fundraiser for over 35 years is to make the world a better place through Philanthropy and guiding families to hand down money wisely and to give strategically. If you would like to explore more about Jesus, this is a resource to begin Bible reading:

Questions about who Jesus is: YouVersion Bible App - YouVersion

To join a small group with others who are exploring faith issues, check out here: http://www.tryalpha.ca/…

www.ingramcontent.com/pod-product-compliance
Lightning Source LLC
Chambersburg PA
CBHW071425220526
45469CB00004B/1435